OBOE

CONCERT FAVORITES

Volume 1

**Band Arrangements Correlated wit[h]
Essential Elements Band Method Book** [1]

ISBN 978-0-634-05200-2

7777 W. BLUEMOUND RD. P.O. BOX 13819 MILWAUKEE, WI 53213

00860120

LET'S ROCK!

OBOE

MICHAEL SWEENEY (ASCAP)

Moderate Rock

Shout:

Let's Rock!

MAJESTIC MARCH

OBOE

By PAUL LAVENDER

March Tempo

00860120

MICKEY MOUSE MARCH
(From Walt Disney's "THE MICKEY MOUSE CLUB")

OBOE

Words and Music by **JIMMIE DODD**
Arranged by **MICHAEL SWEENEY**

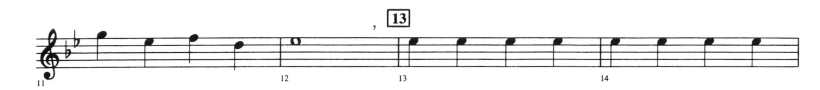

POWER ROCK

(We Will Rock You • Another One Bites The Dust)

OBOE

Arranged by MICHAEL SWEENEY

00860120

WHEN THE SAINTS GO MARCHING IN

Words by KATHERINE E. PURVIS
Music by JAMES M. BLACK
Arranged by JOHN HIGGINS

OBOE

FARANDOLE
(From "L'Arlésienne")

OBOE

GEORGES BIZET
Arranged by MICHAEL SWEENEY (ASCAP)

00860120

JUS' PLAIN BLUES

OBOE

MICHAEL SWEENEY (ASCAP)

From the Paramount and Twentieth Century Fox Motion Picture TITANIC

MY HEART WILL GO ON

(Love Theme From 'Titanic')

Music by JAMES HORNER
Lyric by WILL JENNINGS
Arranged by PAUL LAVENDER

OBOE

Moderately

From THE MUPPET MOVIE

THE RAINBOW CONNECTION

Words and Music by PAUL WILLIAMS
and KENNITH L. ASCHER
Arranged by PAUL LAVENDER

OBOE

From Walt Disney's MARY POPPINS

SUPERCALIFRAGILISTICEXPIALIDOCIOUS

Words and Music by
RICHARD M. SHERMAN and ROBERT B. SHERMAN
Arranged by MICHAEL SWEENEY

OBOE

0860120

OBOE

(FROM "THE SOUND OF MUSIC")
DO-RE-MI

Lyrics by OSCAR HAMMERSTEIN II
Music by RICHARD RODGERS
Arranged by PAUL LAVENDER

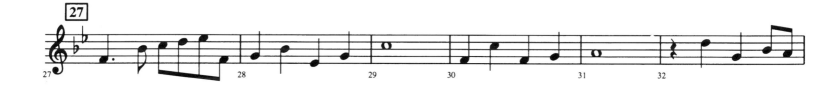

OBOE

MICHAEL SWEENEY (ASCAP)

0860120

LAREDO
(Concert March)

OBOE

JOHN HIGGINS

March No. 1

OBOE

By EDWARD ELGAR
Arranged by MICHAEL SWEENEY

Majestically

5 *Play on repeat only*

13

21

Play both times **29**

37

1. Optional repeat to measure 5

2. Optional repeat to measure 29

3.

STRATFORD MARCH

OBOE

JOHN HIGGINS (ASCA